The Equine Entrepreneur
Your Guide to Building a Profitable Horse Business

Corinna M.W. Charlton

Encouragement
Congratulations on taking action to learn more about your horse business so you can see it grow! There is a lot of material included in this Guide, so I encourage you to focus on your biggest questions first, and go directly to the Mission that will help you the most. You do not have to read this book in numerical order, you can choose your own path to success by jumping straight to the answers to your biggest concerns. Want more support, information, and community? Come find us at RibbonsandRedTape.blogspot.com: navigating the Red Tape of the legal and business world to put your horse business in the Ribbons.

The Equine Entrepreneur Guide

The Equine Entrepreneur Guide

The life of an entrepreneur is not an easy journey. Not only must you learn the technicalities of law and business, you also have to manage finances, time management, marketing and growth, sales, and industry compliance. And many of us are "solopreneurs," which means we are trying to learn how to do all of this well, all on our own. First impressions are important, and the way you present your brand, your customer service, and your product should be at their very possible best from the very beginning.

If you have the time while launching and growing your equestrian venture, possibly while you take on other paying work until your new business can support you, there are often local community small business groups that can be a support network for you. But if you live in a rural area, have very little spare time to join a group, or have an online business, then you are likely searching for that support online. It can be hard to know which group is the right one for you, and whether the group can give you the answers you need to get the most effective results for your horse business. This Guide is a starting point to help you frame the development of your equine business, whether you are in the first stages of business conception or whether you are looking to grow your stagnant sales. The principles and action steps, called Missions in this Guide, will help your individual business. The Missions in this book stem from questions and dilemmas of small and large businesses alike, and the action steps can help you achieve your first sale, or your thousandth.

When you are an equine entrepreneur making money quickly is paramount. Particularly if you are responsible for feeding hungry horses then you need to know which avenue in your business to pursue first in order to turn the earliest profit. Or if you work in the horse division of a company, you likely have limited time to prove to your employers that pursuing the horse market is worthwhile. And the proof is most readily measured in dollars.

This Guide is written from my own experience in the trenches. I am an equine attorney and the author of Ribbons and Red Tape, the equestrian's online resource for education and inspiration on equine law and business. It is my mission to help equip and support the horse community, particularly horse business owners. I offer my free blog resources to help horse people build a better business. A better business involves, among many things, a strong legal foundation, liability savviness, and growth in customer base. I developed this Guide after working directly with equine entrepreneurs who were seeking guidance and support in utilizing their online presence to maximize their audience reach, and correspondingly, their profits. I think the margins and the return on investment from engaging with the online world are superior to any other form of branding and marketing.

When you are a busy equestrian you likely don't have the time to spend hours researching the latest online marketing information, to learn how to use all the different social media tools- or even know which ones you should be using for your particular market- and on top of it, you likely feel very alone as you strive to send your message to the horse world. If you have felt that way, I have been in your shoes. I would watch other business owners collaborate with each other online, cross-promote, and help each other sky rocket in growth. I frequently felt left out or left behind, until I made the deliberate decision to apply my legal and business knowledge to the online world. I know how overwhelming the online world can be, and I wrote this Guide to help support you as you grow your horse business on an online platform. As my disclaimer notes, nothing in this Guide is intended as legal advice. For legal advice in your business you should seek the counsel of an attorney in your jurisdiction. This Guide is written to share the examples of how other equine entrepreneurs have successfully grown their horse businesses and to help prompt your horse business growth with proven action steps.

From both my experience and my experience facilitating exclusive membership groups, I have highlighted 13 Mission Steps for the horse business owner to accomplish to help meet business goals. One or more of these Missions may be a stumbling block, issue, or fear that you have in growing your horse business online. Identify the Mission(s) you need to accomplish and then take steps to overcome and conquer whatever it is reining in your horse business' success!

You will find this guide organized around three principles:

1. *Identification of the Mission*
2. *Explanation of how to break through and accomplish the Mission*
3. *A specific action step for the Mission that will help your unique horse business reach its goals*

A word on Action Steps: knowing the first step you need to

take to meet your horse business goals can break your stagnation. If you feel frozen by the overwhelming amount of work that faces your business, start with these small but highly effective steps forward. My action steps have been applied by many horse business owners with PROVEN results. Whether you are seeking a greater sense of direction with your brand, assistance in creatively growing the dimensions of your business, or seeking increased profit, these Action Steps will provide you with positive results in the pursuit of your goals. I can assure you that the more you put into your horse business, the more you will yield in your horse life, community, and business.

ONE: WHO IS MY IDEAL CLIENT?

When you have a product or service to offer you must consider the following formula:
MY SKILLS + CUSTOMER NEED = PROFIT

Like many people, you are certainly a multi-dimensional person. You have a number of different skills to offer in exchange for client compensation. I imagine you also have skills and abilities that you did not even know were profitable. I suggest you follow a basic two step approach when analyzing who your target market or client base is for your horse business:

1. Identify what prospective customers would be willing to pay for
2. Narrow your skill offerings to reach your ideal customer

As you can see, everything in business ownership revolves around the customer. Until you are compensated for what you do by a customer, your horse business is merely a hobby, and not truly a business. The only way you will be paid is if someone finds your offerings so valuable they are willing to part with their hard-earned money. Your priority is to develop a product or service that *is* valuable, and then convey its value to a prospective purchaser.

In the perfect world, who would purchase your horse product or service? That is your ideal client. But if your sales are sluggish and you are challenged in identifying your ideal client, create one to three client profiles, often called client avatars. Identify at a minimum:

1. What is my ideal client's age range?
2. What is my ideal client's income?
3. Number of children? Number of horses, dogs, cats?
4. What type of riding is my ideal client interested in?
5. What other hobbies does my client have?

To illustrate this problem-solving process, here is an example that would be applicable for horse service providers. My friend is a personal trainer and she told me that her evening sessions were booked with clients but that she needed to find an angle to fill her afternoon spots. She told me that her target market was moms. And not only just moms, but specifically moms who don't work a traditional 8-5 job in a corporate office, moms who would have time for a training session before picking the kids up from school, or moms who can take a personal fitness break while someone stays at home during the children's nap time, such as a family member or nanny.

A horse trainer who works at a barn can problem solve in the same way. You need to fill your dead time with your ideal client. If you teach lessons, identify what you can do to appeal to a client that can fill your time. Or consider what other type of ideal client you can take to fill that time, such as a client who will pay you not for a lesson, but to school his or her horse for a forty-five minute segment.

Identifying the ideal client is also crucial for horse product businesses. If you wish to increase the number of people ordering your product, very specifically identify the profile of the people who already purchase your products. What you know about them can help you expand your reach to a wider client base.

Consider, for example, that your current customers are in the age and lifestyle range where they will soon add children to their families. In this case, you likely want to preempt their demand with creating a marketing plan, and perhaps a product line, appropriate for those customers. They may purchase your products for their own children, or they may be in search of gift ideas for their friends' baby showers or children birthday parties.

The more you learn the details about your existing clients, the more you can anticipate what revenue streams your business needs to pursue in marketing and/or product development.

In conclusion, creating an ideal client helps you market to your present audience better *and* expand your product or service offerings to a great audience   Creating your ideal client avatar requires your creativity in part, but also ASKING your existing clients about themselves and what their needs are. If you have an active fan base on social media, ask for feedback directly. Ask them about their other pets and their families and how those relate to their horse life. For example, 'does your horse like your dog?' And use an image of a horse and dog interacting with each other.   Or use a survey to your audience and existing clients. You can ask things like, "if you had an extra hour at the barn, how would you spend it?" Your ideal client avatar is 1. just getting to know the dimensions of your customer's life better and 2. asking them how their horse lives could be improved through different product or service offerings.

Action Step: Create three specific "ideal client avatars," at a minimum answering the five questions above.

TWO: WHAT ARE THE PERFECT PRODUCTS OR PROGRAMS TO SELL?

Many horse business owners feel frozen or stagnant in their business growth. They know that what they offer is superior to the competitors in the market, and they are confused or frustrated why their products or services aren't selling like hotcakes. Or your brain might be bursting with dozens of different income ideas and you don't know which one to monetize first. Whether you are already in business but feel stagnant, or whether you don't know which idea to pursue first, you must be able to identify the perfect product or program for your audience. Without people who want to buy what you offer, you do not have a viable horse business.

Did you know that people are always telling you what it is they want to buy from you? You just have to learn to listen in the right way.

There is a popular saying in sales psychology, "sell them what they want, and give them what they need." People tend to buy on emotion, though they use reason to rationalize their purchase. So you are selling customers something they emotionally desire, and then your product delivers education or experience that meets or exceeds their needs.

A common purchasing emotion is fear or confusion. Consider the rider who has just gotten a new horse. The rider may be overwhelmingly excited about her new green prospect, and her excitement leads her to take lessons with a new trainer. Or, the rider is happy about her new horse, but is not sure how to train the horse in a particular discipline, or how to continue training the horse in what it already knows how to do. She may fear her inability to keep or maintain the horse's value, and she may fear doing something that will mess-up the horse. That fear or uncertainty will drive her to find resources to help her feel confident moving forward. Those resources may be a new trainer or clinician, or it may be purchasing a horse training course or book. You need to position yourself so that the resources a potential customers seeks lead to you and your business.

The emotion of excitement, fear, or uncertainty in our example is what drives the rider to become a shopper and a buyer, and she will rationalize her purchase by believing that it will increase her positive experience with her horse, which may be a better partnership with her horse in general or winning more at shows. She may also rationalize her purchase by realizing that the information will improve her horse's training so that she doesn't decrease the value of the horse she just purchased, and the resource may even increase the value of her horse for purpose of selling it in the near or distant future.

In essence, many buyers can be viewed like a pre-teen young

adult. A teenager just *has* to have the latest and greatest product or experience (shoes, concert tickets, etc.) and then she justifies her emotion to convince her parents to make the purchase (I need new shoes anyway; I am new at school and this concert will help me make more friends).

Your perfect product or program is a resource that needs to appeal to both the emotional and the rational of the customer's buying impulse. Without a doubt, your perfect product or service also needs to provide incredible value so that your customer is fairly served, and so that your customer eagerly refers your product to her network of friends and family, or perhaps even her larger platform such as a blog.

So, are your listening to what your client is telling you he or she wants to buy? Your perfect product or service will be a direct response to what your ideal customer wants and needs. You need to be a part of the community of your customers, you need to listen and engage to the clues they are giving you as you create your business products and services. If your client is a mom and suffers from lack of time at the barn, make sure you let her know that you offer special grooming or training services at a discounted rate when a rider or horse is enrolled in your training program. Or that you offer shorter lessons if purchased in bulk for the time-pressed equestrian. It is amazing how much can be learned in a 20 minute lesson! Require that the client purchase a package of 10 in order to qualify for the shorter lessons (at a reduced price), request that she warm-up her horse ahead of time, and ask that she refer your special program to other busy riding moms that she knows.

If you are a horse product company, listen to the conversations and complaints of your customer network during different seasons. If they have particular issues or concerns based on winter weather or summer weather, or issues with organization or cleanliness of their horse items at a horse show, adjust your product offerings accordingly. You can create product that adjusts to those issues, and you can also specifically identify how your product or service helps resolve those issues in your marketing plan and the sales funnel of your horse business.

Action Step: Join three new groups where your customer, and prospective customers, can be found. This may be local organizations or it may be online platforms. LinkedIn, Facebook, Google+, and more all have groups specific to your audience. Once you join, authentically engage in building relationships with other members of this group. This will not only help you build trust and credibility in your field, but will also allow you to hear and respond to what problem your customer needs solved in his or her horse life. This will help you create and market a better product or service for your clients.

THREE: WHAT WILL EARN THE MOST MONEY THE FASTEST?

One of the great beauties of being in the entrepreneurial horse business is the ability to maximize multiple income streams. This means that you can earn income from a variety of different avenues: either direct, residual, or passive income.

Direct income is your one to one ratio of work to earnings. For example, if you teach a lesson for one hour, you get paid from that student for that one hour of your time. Residual income is when you work hard to create one product or service and then sell it to many different customers. Passive income is a bit of a misnomer, because all income requires some level of oversight or management. However, passive income can often be seen as collecting dividends from stocks, rental income from property managed by someone else, or perhaps advertising dollars on your horse website or on the walls of your arena, or in the prize list/ program at the show or clinic that you host.

When starting or growing your horse business it is easy to feel defeated when your goals are not met on your timetable. If your website traffic is not growing despite your efforts, your social media fan base is stagnant, you aren't getting new customers, and the bottom line- *you aren't making enough money*. Making money is important, otherwise you should consider pursuing your passion and vision as a hobby and not as a business.

Making money quickly is important for horse business owners, to cover the costs of starting-up such as incorporating or purchasing software; to cover the costs of overhead such as leasing stable space for your horse training business; to feed you and your family; and to encourage you to keep pushing forward with your business. When you are rewarded for your efforts, this not only is immensely gratifying on a personal level, but on a practical level it allows you to stay in business.

I know that some horse online business owners put Google Adwords on their site in desperation to just get some money. Unless your traffic is substantial, such as 20,000 unique visitors to your site per month, then Google Adwords will likely yield only pennies, perhaps a few dollars each month. I think this may be a waste of your time and of your brand integrity. There are of course various success stories out there that contradict my opinion- and if you generate a worthwhile income stream from Google Adwords then that is fantastic! In general, I think your efforts can be better placed elsewhere. And your efforts should go towards creating your Minimally Viable Product.

A Minimally Viable Product is a product or service you can create and complete quickly. This product should be substantial enough and offer sufficient value that customers would be willing to purchase. If your goal is to write a 500 page book about your unique horse training methods, a book that is a complete and thorough explanation of your life's work with horses, complete with diagrams and pictures, that is most likely *not* your Minimally Viable Product. Such a book would presumably take a minimum of six months of intensive work, and some people take years to create such a product. My opinion is that your Minimally Viable Product needs to be created, designed, packaged, and available for sale within thirty days.

A Minimally Viable Product is a product or service

you can create and complete quickly.

If you are a service provider in the horse industry, such as selling your expertise or training or consulting or convenience services (like equestrian-specific bookkeeping), consider what is the shortest path to your first dollar. Be prepared: the shortest path may not be something you enjoy, or that you wish to become your primary form of income. However, once you start moving forward with your first ten, one hundred, or one thousand dollars, you will have the energy and freedom to pursue paths that have longer yields to income. You will also build your confidence and belief in your business.

For example, your passion is to focus on equestrian bookkeeping because you love to help manage the cash flow of large boarding barns. You get excited about managing and advising on hay delivery, training programs, rehabilitation income possibilities, and you eventually want to create specific software or literature to sell to other equestrian bookkeepers or to boarding barns to create a residual income stream. However, your client list is minimal and it will take 6-12 months to create your software or literature. That means you must find the Minimally Viable Product to start earning your first dollars as an equine bookkeeper business owner. While you may not enjoy creating and filing tax returns for small horse businesses, because it is tax season there are five clients that you can help right now, and you need to do that. Or, if you are working on developing proprietary equestrian bookkeeping software while you continue to work in your day job, then you should create and sell your initial e-book about equestrian bookkeeping while you create your software.

This will help build your brand and authority in the field, it will help you start building your audience of people interested in your expertise, and it will allow you an avenue to receive feedback from customers who purchase your e-book, which may be invaluable as you create your software.

The world needs to know you are in business. If you have nothing offered for sale, then you are missing an opportunity to build your reputation as the best source for your equestrian expertise.

Action Step: Identify the three goals you hope to develop in your business that will take 6-12 months to complete. Now, break each of those goals into smaller steps or products to create the Minimally Viable Product.

FOUR: HOW DO I RECEIVE FEEDBACK?

It is a truth of life and business that money is a motivator. I believe you are reading this Guide because you have an important message or mission to share with the horse community. And I believe you are also reading this because you know there is the potential for greater monetization of your message, but you are not making the progress that you know you are capable of achieving. I believe money is important! It is a motivator and an affirmation that your business is the RIGHT avenue for your valuable time and effort. A hard truth: some businesses should not be continued. In some cases, the business owner should cut her losses because the business is a bad idea for any number of reasons. Ultimately, in my opinion, sales are the only feedback that matters when you are creating a business to make money. This may be tough love for you to hear, yet if all your family and friends rave about your business idea, you are in love with your business idea, but *no one is buying your service or produc*t? You should consider folding and moving to your next idea.

Sales are the ONLY feedback that matters.

But take heart, there are things you can do to increase your sales. One of the most important steps you can take is to receive feedback on your horse product or business. There are two types of feedback that you should seek:

1. Feedback from Collaborators

A collaborator is someone who is also in business. They do

not need to be in the same type of business as you, and in fact, diversity in the field of business can provide great value. If you sell horse products, find a collaborator who sells horse services. The root of your marketing will collectively be the same, selling to the equestrian industry, but your varied experiences will help you collaborate together.

Realize that collaboration is most gainful when it is a two-way street. This helps build relationship, trust, and respect. If you ask another horse business owner to review your website design, be willing also to review the other business owner's website or product design. From this relationship will emerge opportunities to help support each other and cross-promote each other's businesses to your respective audiences.

One of the best ways to receive collaborative feedback is to join a group specifically facilitated to serve horse business owners, or other business owners in general. I find a lot of value from being a member of horse business groups on platforms like LinkedIn, and non-equine/ general business groups on various platforms because I can continue to learn from other business fields. I also facilitate horse business mastermind groups to bring together collaborators seeking to give and receive feedback.

A mastermind group is most effective when it is a small group of highly motivated business owners who are energetic to improve their businesses effectively and quickly, and to help serve other horse business owners along the way by offering encouragement, technical advice, and cross-promotion and support. The online world is enormous and can often feel isolating or lonely; being an active member of a business group will allow you an avenue to authentic and quality feedback from business owners who are tackling the same legal, marketing, sales, and product development questions that you have in your own business.

2. Feedback from Clients and Customers

This is an entirely different type of feedback than that from collaborators, but it is crucial feedback that you must continually seek and use in your horse business. You need to receive feedback from the audience that is purchasing your product or service. If they love what they bought then you need to know! Not only will it encourage you, but you can also use their positive experience as testimonials when marketing your horse business to other audiences and potential clients. If you are selling a horse training book, a handful of testimonials that attest to the book's value can help persuade other shoppers to purchase your book as well.

Feedback from present customers can also show you room for improvement. We all hate to hear what our product or service is lacking- after all- we have poured our hearts, money, and time into our horse business and to hear negativity can be hurtful or demoralizing. However, when you approach your audience with the prompt, "I want to serve you better, what improvement or change or addition would you like to see from my horse service or product?" then you can understand your customer base better and improve your business constructively rather than based on negativity.

If you teach horse lessons, you may receive a request for more group lessons, a more flexible lesson schedule, or a payment plan to help with the rider's budgeting. **Be open-minded when you receive these suggestions, and be grateful! Your customers are telling you exactly what to do to KEEP them as a customer.** When a customer feels you are responsive to her needs she is more likely to be a satisfied customer- and satisfied customers are more likely to tell their network about you and your business. If you can even over-deliver based on a customer's request for change, you will create a brand with a shining reputation for customer service and product or service quality.

Feedback can be received in a variety of different ways, and is largely dependent on the type of business that you have. If you primarily have an in-person business, such as teaching students, then feedback can be received through conversation. If you ask your existing client what you can do differently, and she feels it is a genuine request that will be safely received (never defensively!), you can then organically generate the general consensus from your customers of what they would like to see from your horse service.

Whether you are a physical or online business I recommend a monthly newsletter to your audience. Your newsletter can contain a survey for feedback- which can be anonymous if you feel clients will respond more readily without revealing their identity. The survey can be as simple or complex as you feel is appropriate, and can even simply ask clients to rank their satisfaction with the customer service, delivery, or quality of what you offer to them. An online search will reveal a number of different paid or unpaid survey services. A popular one is SurveyMonkey.com.

If you ask your readership to respond to a survey or for answers to your questions and find participation is low, consider providing an incentive for their responses. Everyone who responds perhaps may receive one complimentary 15 minute coaching or training session or a free copy of your e-book; or depending on the number of responses you anticipate, the responders will be entered to win a gift card, lesson package, or other incentive. Always be sure that giveaways or contests comply with federal and your state laws. You can read more about that in the Ribbons and Red Tape blog post, *"How to Avoid a Horse Giveaway that Breaks the Law."*

Action Step: This week, seek feedback from three collaborators and three customers or potential customers. Ask what is appreciated about your horse business, and ask what can be improved. Ask potential customers why they chose not to buy at this time, and what you can do to provide better value in the future.

FIVE: HOW DO I FIND TIME TO WORK ON MY HORSE BUSINESS WHILE KEEPING MY DAY JOB?

Time: we all have the same amount, but many of us never seem to have enough! We all have 168 hours each week. It is extraordinary what some people accomplish with those 168 hours, and how little others are able to get done in the same amount of time.

My general rule of thumb of honesty with myself is to never say, "I don't have enough time to do that," but to say, "it was not a priority for me to get that done." This can hit a raw chord in the busy business owner, as well as the business owner's family and friends. You can imagine the conversations:

"Why didn't you make it to our family Thursday night dinner?"

"It wasn't a priority for me on Thursday evening."

"Did you call your sick mother today?"
  "No, it wasn't a priority."

As many people say, "we make time for what we want to do." This requires that we closely prioritize all the responsibilities we have in life. If your 40 hour a week day job is a priority because it is the only income that feeds and provides health care for your family, then you certainly need to make time to perform that job well.

When you plan your 168 hours per week, deduct your 40 hour day job and the time you need to sleep, exercise, and spend time with your children, spouse, or other important family members. Sleep and family relationships are crucial to your emotional, mental, and spiritual well-being and will make you more effective and productive pursuing your dream horse business.

After this prioritizing, find the gaps where you are losing time or would be able to reduce time. If the time you spend with your spouse tends to be dinner then a 45 minute television show, you should consider forfeiting the television show and focusing more on the time you have to talk with your spouse over dinner. If you work out at a gym that is a fifteen minute drive away each way for an hour long yoga class, consider dropping your gym membership and doing yoga or exercise at home with a guided series. You will save driving time, the long class time, and the mysterious minutes that slip away in-between.

If you are serious about growing your horse business while maintaining your day job then you need to be serious about the sacrifices you need to make, which include the luxury of wasted time.

Without a sacrifice you will never have the opportunity to work in your horse business full time

Fortunately, a great amount can be accomplished in your horse business if you mentally commit to intense and focused bursts of energy in your project. If you have committed to producing your

Minimally Viable Product, then you need to accomplish that task as quickly and efficiently as possible. If you take a lunch break at work, and your Minimally Viable Product is an e-book, then draft your table of contents during your break. That table of contents will become the outline for the book. Make it a priority over the next one or two weeks to complete one chapter a day or every few days. Weekends are often filled with horse shows and clinics and lazy afternoons at the barn, but make it a priority to get highly focused bursts of work accomplished in the development of your product or service. You may need to wake up an hour or two earlier on the weekends to focus on your horse business over coffee. You may need to spend less time with your horse in order to work on your dream horse business.

These certainly are sacrifices, but realize that without a sacrifice you will never have the opportunity to work in your horse business full time. Without the sacrifice you will not create a viable additional income stream (if you wish to stay in your day job). And know that with the sacrifice you will yield results that far exceed your expectations. You may know the saying, "Failing to plan means planning to fail." Without a doubt I empathize how impossible it seems to balance a day job, family life, horses, and growing your horse business. But with a positive mindset and aggressive planning, scheduling, and sacrifice, it is also without a doubt that you will break through this stage and will experience success in starting and growing your horse business.

Online businesses have a particular advantage because they are free from restraints of normal business hours. Your blog posts and social media posts can be scheduled for the hours your customers will be online, even if you are creating the post at ten at night. Most blog platforms have built in tools for scheduling posts, and there are a number of third-party sites that will schedule your social media posts to go out at particular times to all the different sites. Even if you are a physical business you can use these online tools to your advantage. For example, by growing your e-mail list you can have direct access to current and prospective clients. You can create your weekly email in bursts of time, and likely can generate 4 weeks of email in one Saturday evening. Schedule them to go out at the same time each day of the week over the next four weeks.

Success tip: tailor these emails to when they will be scheduled on the calendar. For example, in the newsletter that will go out three weeks from now identify what horse show, event, or national holiday will occur that week. If something extraordinary happens in your business after you create your month of emails then you can take one minute or less to log in to your email server, add an update into the already created newsletter of the big show win or press your business received, helping ensure that your big news make it out to your email audience in a timely manner.

If you are financially able, you may want to consider hiring a contractor to help you meet the demands of your life. If your horse business needs website content written, consider outsourcing it to a copywriter or virtual assistant who charges an hourly rate within your budget. There are a number of different sites where these virtual assistants can be found.

Action Step: 1) identify where you are losing time in your day- either time that is unaccounted for in your schedule, such as the thirty minutes after you get home from work- or activities that can survive a reduction in time spent on them. 2) Create your list of priorities and ensure that your horse business is included as one of the most essential activities in your life (job and family are most likely your highest priorities) and the specific time windows in your week that you can spend on your horse business, then bring your family on board to help you commit to that schedule.

SIX: HOW CAN I CREATE A FINANCIAL CUSHION TO QUIT MY DAY JOB?

If you are currently working on salary with benefits, the idea of stepping full time in your horse business can be frightening. For some, the decision is made for you: you are laid off, you follow a spouse to a new town, or the demands in your life make it impossible to continue to work for your present office. For others, the step into financial insecurity is frightening. So frightening that it can even be immobilizing and prevent you from pursuing your business with the energy and focus you know it needs to take it to the next level.

There are two main ways to tackle the transition in pay. First, you can work on your horse business on the side of your job. At a certain point there is enough money coming in that the step into entrepreneurship and financial self-reliance is balanced enough between risk and reward. You have confidence that the money you earn while only focusing on your horse business on the side will only increase once you focus on your business full time. For example, you have a long wait-list of clients or customers who are demanding your service or product, but until you quit your day job, you will not be able to serve them. This is a great scenario to be in!

Just have a plan of action.

The second primary way entrepreneurs manage the financial switch from full time salary to paying themselves out of their business is a bridge job. A bridge job is one that offers flexibility, and often wages below what you would otherwise receive in your field for your experience. A bridge job is often one in which you are a part time employee or an independent contractor so that you can spend more time in your horse business while still receiving cash flow until your business can support you.

The bridge job that is best for you depends on your age, skills, and comfort level. There are many entrepreneurs in their twenties who have worked as waiters while they build their business. Others are freelance journalists and are able to write enough to earn money to support them while they build their dream horse company. You may choose to teach summer riding camp for children while you work on your horse business in developing online riding lesson modules.

I think a bridge job is a worthwhile option if it offers you enough time and enough money to allow you to put the attention into your horse business that it needs. Arguably, a bridge job could be better for launching your business rather than while comfortably employed because you will be hungrier for the success of your horse business. For some people, the desire to leave a bridge job is fuel on the entrepreneurial fire to make their dream business and lifestyle a reality as soon as possible.

That being said, I also think it ideal if you can work a bridge job in a similar field as your horse business. This may or may not be restricted to working with horses. As in my example above, if you want to create and sell riding instruction online videos, then teaching horse riding camp will keep you passionate and motivated for your endeavor- and connected to an audience that could become customers. However, if you want to build your riding apparel business, your bridge job may be in a mainstream or local retail store. This will allow you to continue to learn what you do and do not want in your own business, even though it isn't strictly equestrian. Or you can waiter, or tutor high school students, or work part-time in a field of your education or training. Just have a plan of action. Know how long you will be in the bridge job. Write down the math of income to expenses of your bridge job and your horse business, and memorize your numbers.

Finally, the best way to build a financial cushion to quit your day job and work full time in your horse business (other than a financial windfall from an inheritance or lottery), is to save every dollar and dime that you can. If you can save enough money to support yourself for one to two years, then you likely have the focus, passion, and drive it will take to make your horse business profitable within that timeframe.

Action Step: if you are working full time in your day job, <u>calculate</u> the amount of money your horse business must be earning to allow you to quit and focus on your horse venture full time. Or, <u>ask</u> your company if you can switch to part-time work so that you have enough money coming in to allow you the security to pursue your horse business with greater focus. Finally, if you wish to work a flexible bridge job, consider which ones would be suitable for your financial and time needs for your life and business and <u>contact</u> three of those options this week regarding a position.

SEVEN: HOW CAN I OVERCOME SELF-DOUBT AND CREATE A BETTER MINDSET FOR MY HORSE BUSINESS?

YOU ARE NOT ALONE. This first and foremost is the most important realization you need to have. You are not the only person that feels overwhelmed with how to grow your horse business, you are not the only person that is confused or fearful, or the only entrepreneur that doubts his or her ability or business idea.

But knowing theoretically that you are not the only one with self doubt is very different than actually feeling assured that you are on the right path, that your horse business idea is a good one, and that your skills and knowledge and offerings are worth the amount of money you are asking customers and clients to pay.

Meet Goals and Ask for Feedback

One of the best ways to assuage self-doubt is to meet and exceed goals you have set for your horse business. If your goal is to double your blog traffic, add 100 new subscribers to your e-mail list, or to make your first sale and you meet that goal, then that affirms you are doing the right thing.

When you follow-up with a new subscriber, service client, or product customer ask what specifically she liked about your horse business product or service, and you are likely to receive positive testimonials. Not only are testimonials valuable for your sales and marketing plan, but it also helps vanquish your self-doubt. People love what your do and are willing to pay for it! You will be on Cloud Nine.

Action Step: re-read this Guide's Mission Four about receiving feedback. Ask one existing client or customer individually what he or she appreciates about your horse business and save that positive testimonial for your own personal encouragement; with permission, you should also use the feedback to promote your

horse business to prospective clients.

Join Motivating Groups
  A common descriptive word in the world of online support groups is your "tribe." A tribe is the group of like-minded business owners you build relationship with for support, encouragement, and shared passion for growing your mission and business. For horse business owners we can similarly say that you need to find your "herd."
  It is always a good idea, but especially crucial if you struggle with self-doubt or business confusion, to join social media groups that have active threads. When a group has an active thread it means the members of the group are regularly posting relevant content and also quickly respond to the questions that you pose to the group. You should join groups that are relevant both to the horse world and to the business world generally. Not only will you have access to learn more about your "ideal customer," but depending on your business model you may also find potential clients or customers in each of those threads.
  You should consider creating or joining small focus groups, often called a Mastermind group. This Mastermind group generally has an accountability structure that encourages you to post your goals and mission, and then take the steps to get there. If you are stuck with which step to take next, the other group members typically jump in to help point you in the right direction and motivate you to keep moving forward. I have found that paid membership sites can be great if you join the one that is right for your personality and the time that you want to spend in your business. A membership site is typically hosted by one or two Internet personalities; someone who has applied online marketing and sales principles to business and then shares that information with all paying members. These paid membership sites generally have forums restricted to other paying members, which can serve as a great place to receive feedback, to learn how other business owners are applying sales and marketing principles, and for you to engage with others who are pushing forward to meet goals.
  One positive aspect of a paid site is the general rule of thumb that if you pay for something you are more invested in the process.

Failure to engage or learn from a paid membership group means you are throwing away money each money. If you are paying for your membership you are financially and psychologically invested in maximizing your membership fee to its full extent- so you will typically make it a greater priority to learn the material being provided and to make relationships with other members.

Whether you decide to join a large or small group, no cost or with a fee, taking the step to join is the important part. Find a group that is active and that you feel comfortable asking and giving feedback. Know what it is that you want out of the group, and be dedicated. The relationships you build and the practical knowledge you gain will help alleviate self-doubt and help you have a positive, entrepreneurial mindset.

Action Step: this week, join three groups that are relevant to your mission, purpose, and horse business. Ask your current "herd" what other business leaders they recommend that you follow or sites that would be valuable for you to join. Consider one LinkedIn Group, one Facebook group, and one paid membership site or Mastermind group of other motivated horse business owners.

Embrace that doubt is good

Being in business for yourself undoubtedly carries risk. It may be financial risk or risk to your reputation. You may be risking a setback in a traditional career path by pursuing your horse business. Doubt is a good thing because it helps you evaluate risk and then apply logic and a system to help alleviate the risk. If you are the sole supporter of a family of three, along with a mortgage and horses, then jumping out of a secure job at the first whim of a business idea is likely not a good idea. You should doubt that decision! However, by acknowledging the doubt you can also move forward in creating a plan in how to alleviate risk and thereby alleviate the doubt. If you begin to build income from your new business venture, have created a financial cushion for your family, and receive positive feedback from other business owners and from paying clients, then the self-doubt should be reduced to the point that taking the risk of leaving the secure job is not only worthwhile, but the best decision that you will ever make.

If pursuing your dream job gives you the freedom and passion that you desire, then you should never allow self-doubt to prevent you from moving forward in launching and growing your horse business. Picture what your horse business would look like with nominal success, and also great success. If you sell custom saddle pads and related horse gear, what would nominal success look like? Perhaps enough sales from the saddle pads to match your current day job salary? And what would great success look like? A lucrative distribution contract with the largest equestrian supplier? Or maybe expanding your offerings and customer base to double or triple your current annual salary?

Would owning your own business give you greater control over your schedule so you can spend more time traveling or more time with your family or at the barn? Envision your dream, wake up every morning excited to pursue that dream and to make it happen as soon as possible. When every fiber of your being wants to see your dream horse business come to fruition, self doubt is relegated a much smaller space in your mindset. If you are passionate about your horse business and creating the life you love, and you continue to teach yourself the tools of maximizing the potential in your horse business (such as by reading books and blogs relevant to growing your business, taking physical or online courses, or joining focus groups or membership sites), then your energy and belief in yourself and in the potential of your horse business will skyrocket.

ACTION STEP: Identify one of your areas of doubt. Reach out to one of the business groups you belong to and share your doubt and ask for suggestions for moving forward. If you are not yet part of a business group (equestrian or otherwise) join one today!

Stop the Comparison Game

You may know the expression, "don't compare your beginning with someone else's middle." First, if you are just starting out in your horse business, do not be disheartened that other similar brands are much larger than yours- larger social media audiences, a better website, or a higher advertising budget. Use those other companies as encouragement, not as a basis to feel inferior. Apply yourself to get out of beginning stages and into the "middle" stage of your business as efficiently as possible. It takes some business owners 6 months to get out of the beginning stages, it takes others 6 years. Create your own timetable and markers of growth for your horse business and keep that as the basis for your comparison. I compare myself on a weekly and monthly basis to assess my growth. I like to see how my traffic, subscribers, and sales change each week. This is valuable comparison because I can track what tactics work, and which ones I need to change. For this reason, every horse business owner needs to have analytic tracking on his or her site. Even if you don't have the time to learn how to read all the data you need to start collecting the data immediately. This is invaluable information when you are deciding how to take your horse business to the next level and to see the effects of your advertising and marketing.

ACTION STEP: Stop visiting websites or blogs that make you feel bad or inferior in your horse business. Commit to only reading or visiting those sites when you either 1) want to specifically see how your competitors are applying marketing or other business tools or 2) you have just celebrated a milestone in your horse business and want to go to the competitor site to be inspired to achieve the next milestone.

Take Note of what is Working

Meeting a goal is the best way to feel a sense of accomplishment and security that what you are doing is working. If you are meeting your profit goals then celebrate! Be sure to reward yourself and to take breaks from your horse business.

Receiving feedback, reviews, and sales is also a great way to take note of what is working in your business.

ACTION STEP: Choose a day each week that you will sit down and deliberately list what went well for your horse business during the week. Even if your sales unexpectedly plummeted or your website crashed, aspire to find the positive in the past week and congratulate yourself for always striving to move forward in

your horse business. If you finish reading a business book, join a new Mastermind group, or meet a mini-goal, know that investing in your business education will yield great results. Completing an Action Step from this Guide is certainly something to celebrate!

EIGHT: HOW DO I KNOW THE RIGHT PRICING FOR MY HORSE BUSINESS SERVICE OR PRODUCT?

The right price for your product or service is the price that your ideal customer is willing and able to pay. While true, what does it mean for your horse business? Answer the following four questions to start forming the right prices you need and want to be charging to your customer base.

1. How much do I aim to make in my horse business this month?
2. Is my product or service something that is sold to many people, or sold to few or limited number of people?
3. Is my horse product or service an item that falls generally into the high or low price end of the market for this good?
4. What are competitors charging for a similar product or service, and what differentiates my horse product or service to affect whether I charge more or less?
5. Those four steps don't help or don't apply to me, and I have no idea what this should cost. What do I do now?

Pricing is an art and a science. Depending on your business model, you should determine whether it is sales in quantity, in quality, or in both that will sustain and grow your business. If you aim to make $1,000.00 next month in your horse business you have to evaluate which of those attribute will help you reach your goal.

For example, if your horse business has an e-mail list of 100 subscribers, then selling each subscriber a $10.00 product will yield you $1,000.00 that month. However, it is statistically unlikely that every subscriber will purchase your product, so you can either increase the price so that 50 of your subscribers are willing to pay $20.00 for the product, or you need to keep the product at $10.00 but increase your e-mail list size so the statistical conversion of your subscriber to a buyer of your product will allow you to reach your $1,000.00 goal.

If you are a horse service provider, such as a horse trainer or farrier, then you are likely limited in the amount of clients you can take. For this reason you would need to focus on maximizing the number of customers you can take (such as group lessons) and you need to focus on generating clients that are willing to pay a higher price so you can meet your monthly profit goal within your limited timeframe.

Split Testing and Tiered Packages

There are two methods of buyer psychology that can help you establish the right price for your product and convert more shoppers into buyers. Split testing and tiered packages are two very different tactics, but they both rely on responding to what your customer is thinking when she is making the decision whether to buy your product or service.

Split testing is most simply understood as creating two or more advertisements, prices, or other images and analyzing which one performs better. For example, you could create two similar Facebook advertisements for your custom horse brow band business and then analyze which advertisement receives more clicks. The goal of split testing is to determine which advertisement is more popular, then you know it is worth putting more money into advertising one image over another. For example, one female entrepreneur with an audience geared towards other females found that Facebook users typically preferred to click her advertisement that had a pink logo over her picture rather than a green or blue logo.

You can use split testing in your horse business in a number of different ways. You can use it with paid advertising, like in the Facebook example above. Or you can use it on your blog to see which advertisement or logo receives more interest, either through clicks or through purchases. Split testing can also be used in pricing, though this is more sophisticated and I see it used typically more with services than horse products. Horse products have fixed margins so there is less flexibility in the price that can be charged, though you may find it interesting if more people purchase an item at $17.00 rather than $19.00. It is an odd phenomenon in the online marketplace that numbers that end in seven often do better from a sales perspective than other numbers!

If you think split testing would be a good fit for you I encourage you to read resources devoted entirely to the subject to learn how to use it, or you may want to hire a contractor to create and track split testing results for you. There are also a number of websites that offer split testing services. For example, Hello Bar is a free e-mail capture tool that embeds across the top of your website. Hello Bar offers free basic split testing to determine traffic popularity and conversions. For example, you can create Hello Bar in two different colors to see which one your traffic responds to better. You can also create bars that have two different opt-in call to actions in them, such as "Receive a 10% discount code on your next purchase when you subscribe" versus "Receive a free gift with purchase when you subscribe." Hello Bar then displays a different bar for different users who come to your site, and from that you can track the analytics to see which color bar or offer opportunity gives rise to greater conversions of a visitor becoming a subscriber.

You can use split testing to determine your pricing when you run a split test of different prices for the same product that is pitched differently. For example, you are offering private coaching for equestrian competitors to help them have more confidence and better vision in their riding goals. Your split test may look as follows:
Advertisement One offers private coaching, emphasizing *gaining more confidence* in the show ring, priced at $499.00.
Advertising Two offers private coaching, emphasizing *winning more frequently* in the show ring, priced at $599.00.

You are selling the same horse service, but you are testing two things in this split test, value to the consumer (addressing a "pain point" that a horseback rider has) and the price. Split testing is likely most valuable when testing only one element at a time, so depending on your goals of the split test- such as color of the advertisement, customer pain point, or the best price for the service- isolate your advertisement accordingly. This will help you understand your ideal customer's psychology better, and you can then shape the rest of your sales and marketing strategy around what you know about your customer's preference.

Tiered packages are a much simpler way to subtly ask your customer what he or she would rather buy from you, and at what price. Tiered packages are two or more products or services that have different prices. A general rule of thumb in human psychology is the desire to choose the median, or middle, option. Therefore if you offer private coaching for equestrian competitors you may have three packages that look like the following:

Package One offers group coaching and general support for 30 days priced at $50.00
Package Two offers group coaching plus 3 private sessions for 30 days priced at $250.00
Package Three offers group coaching plus 10 private sessions for 30 days priced at $750.00

By using tiered packages you can determine what your customer values the most. When you know what the customer values you can then offer more of that product or service. In this example you will identify whether customers prefer a particular price point, or whether it is private sessions that are more important. The tiered packaging approach allows you to test what price is the right price for your services because you can respond to what your customers are buying. If 90% of your customers purchase the $50.00 package then you can adjust your sales and marketing to draw more customers into the group coaching at that price point.

Price Confidence
One of the hardest aspects for the horse business owner is the willingness to charge what your product or service is worth. Especially when we are just starting in the business it is difficult to believe that people will be willing to exchange their hard-earned money for what you have to offer. If you struggle with confidence in believing people will pay you for your skill, knowledge, or product offerings then consider two paths: charge less or push

forward.

If you are testing your market and fear not being able to get enough customers at the price you would like to charge consider offering limited time offers for a reduced price. You do not want to establish a precedent of selling your product or service for 50% less than what you feel you deserve. However, if it is important to you to begin making some income quickly from your horse business and to start receiving feedback from customers, offering a reduced price for a limited number of individuals or for a limited amount of time could be a strategy to boost your confidence.

Bundle your horse product or service to increase the value to the customer without reducing the advertised price of your product.

To avoid discounting your price you may also wish to bundle your horse product or service to increase the value to the customer without reducing the advertised price of your product. Once a price is established it can be difficult to later convince the consumer to purchase the same product or service at a higher price. Therefore consider offering your $99.99 custom horse purse made with authentic halter parts with a bonus custom colored lead rope. Tell your customer that this lead rope is normally a $24.99 value, but for a limited time with the purchase of the purse the lead rope will be included. This type of bundling promotion maintains the price point of the purse, offers the customer an additional value, and creates a sense of urgency that customers will only receive this promotion for a limited amount of time. Use promotions sparingly with the deliberate purpose of generating cash flow and customer reviews. If you are known as always offering promotions then customers may not be motivated or feel a sense of urgency to make a purchase because they anticipate another promotion coming soon.

If you do not wish to reduce your price at all, if you do not have bundling promotion available or think it unadvisable for your product or service, and you know that your horse product or service is worth its asking price (if not more) then push ahead into your fear. Establish a baseline goal of how many customers or clients you want for your new horse business product or service at your price, then do everything possible to meet that baseline goal. Imagine the joy of exceeding your goal! Envision success, create your plan, and re-evaluate your goal or your price only when necessary.

For example, if you know your private coaching for equestrian competitors is worth $499.00 for group and 3 sessions of one on one consulting, then keep that price and confidence and go out and get those customers. Be committed to having five new clients sign up for that package (tiered packages is likely still advisable), and tirelessly commit to meeting that goal at that price point. You are in your business because you have a passion for your mission, you know you have the skills and/or product to add value to customers, and you deserve to receive a fair profit for your hard work, investment, and expertise. So price it accordingly and pursue your goal!

ACTION STEP: Determine what dollar amount you want to make from your horse business this month and decide to use one or all of the following pricing methods: limited time or customer price discounting promotion; bundling of your full-priced product or service; tiered packaging. Also, if split-testing interests you, read three resources on the topic that offers you further in-depth knowledge.

NINE: HOW DO I CREATE AN EFFECTIVE SALES FUNNEL?

A Sales Funnel is the process of turning a casual visitor into a buying customer. Sales Funnels tie in with our later sections on product launches and creative ways to drive sales, so this section will offer an introductory overview of how sales funnels are best utilized in your horse business.

Truly internalize that you have something incredibly

valuable or great to offer to the horse community.

The idea of "selling" can be met with mixed reactions. On the one hand, you do not have a business if you do not have anyone buying your product or service. On the other hand, a lack of confidence or a general negative perception of being "salesy" can prevent business owners from reaching out to their equestrian audience.

The first important step is to truly internalize that you have something incredibly valuable or great to offer to the horse community. Whether it is your unique coaching method, horse training tips, a new form of equestrian apparel or grooming supplies, you have a product or service that you know horse people need and would love. With that in mind, you need to also understand that your product or service has taken your skill, time, effort, and investment to create. For that reason, you need to receive value in exchange for the value you are providing. For most business owners, this value is money. In the previous section we learned about establishing *Pricing* for your horse product or service, so now your focus needs to be "funneling" the horse community to your product.

A sales funnel relies on two things: awareness and compulsion.

Awareness

Horse owners or riders need to know that your product or service exists. Especially in the age of online marketing there are many ways to reach prospective customers. You can use your audience on social media, the traffic to your blog or website, and your e-mail list (if you haven't already started building your e-mail list, this is crucial!) to announce your latest offering.

You can also cross-promote with other horse business owners or equestrian sites. Cross-promoting is most effective when it springs from relationship. As a member of various horse sites you have had the opportunity to create relationship with individuals or other horse entities. Reach out to these various people or businesses to let them know what you are offering, and why you think it would be of value to them or to their audience and readers. By doing so you not only receive an expressed or implied referral from others, but you also gain access to their own list and traffic.

There are of course paid efforts that can help you reach your ideal customer base. First, Facebook advertising can be highly effective because you can target your prospective audience in very specific ways. Advertising your new course or product in the sidebar of particular horse websites or blogs can also help you reach an audience that is predisposed to become your customer. Finally, using search engine advertising can be effective, particularly if you have a product or service that lends itself to search words, such as "custom dressage brow band."

Affiliate marketing could be described as a blend between free and paid advertising. Affiliate marketing can be shaped in different ways, but essentially allows someone who promotes your product or service to receive a portion of the proceeds for each customer who buys through the promoters link to your horse business. This can have the benefit of reaching a focused audience as well as an implied or express endorsement of your horse product or service by the affiliate party, though you do suffer a cut to your profit when you pay affiliate proceeds. You need to determine what margins you need for your horse business to decide whether affiliate marketing might be a right start for your sales funnel.

A funnel is widest at the top, and this is where your efforts towards audience awareness begin the journey through the sales funnel. Maximize the amount of awareness, or the quality of the traffic, at the very beginning of your sales process.

Compulsion

Generally it is easier to get someone to buy your horse service or product if they are already committed to your horse business. If they read your blog, follow you on social media, and are an e-mail subscriber then they likely have a positive mindset towards what your horse business offers. Establishing this sense of trust, continuity, and relationship with your horse business and free content is an important part of the sales funnel.

If you have tiered pricing for your products or services then focus on moving someone who enjoys your free content to someone who has made a first purchase on your site. Focus on getting the mere observers who visit your site to purchase your most affordable item. This may be a \$4.99 product or service, but it is not the money you earn from the item that is most important, but shifting your relationship with the customer from one who consumes your free material as a reader to one who is actually a customer. If that customer has a positive experience in his or her purchase of your service or product then the customer is more likely to subsequently purchase a higher-priced item. As your sales funnel narrows to your expensive offerings, it is inevitable that the number of ideal customers ready, willing, and able to purchase that item will shrink. But if you can sell to someone once, it is easier to sell to him again. Once you learn the motivating factors of your customers you can more effectively move them forward towards the purchase you would like them to make.

In your sales funnel, focus on turning cold traffic (people who visit your site once) into warm traffic (becoming an e-mail subscriber) into warmer traffic (by purchasing your most affordable offering), into hot traffic- those customers who buy everything you offer and excitedly share your horse business with everyone they know because they are such big believers in your product or service.

ACTION STEP: Identify what stage of the sales funnel you need to improve. If you need to grow awareness, take action by asking other horse people or business owners to help promote your business, product, or service. If you need to grow compulsion to buy, develop a lower priced product or service to convert warm traffic who consume your free content into warmer traffic willing to enter into a merchant relationship with you.

TEN: HOW DO I CREATE AN EFFECTIVE PRODUCT LAUNCH?

Product launches have received a huge amount of attention with the growth of online platforms and sales. Physical businesses, such as tack stores, use traditional methods of product launches, such as mailing postcards to prospective customers, paying for advertisements in relevant magazines, or putting banners up across the storefront. The growth of the online audience renders it vital to implement your launch in an online space if you wish to reach as many people as possible.

Product launches are ways of alerting an audience that your horse business has a new product or service available. Online product launches can be viewed as virtual implementation of traditional methods of product launches, such as online "open houses," where your online community is invited to your barn or tack shop website for various festivities and free door prizes.

You need to view your product launch as a focused and intense sales funnel.

Product launches in the online world have become an elaborate science of marrying numerous tools and marketing methods to make the biggest splash possible when presenting a new product to the online world. In brief, you need to view your product launch as a focused and intense sales funnel. If you are selling a horse product or service that begins on a particular date or will be available for only a limited amount of time, use this timeline to create a sense of urgency with your audience. If you are launching a new item that does not have a sense of urgency, and you may consider creating a bonus item to sell with your new product or service to help jumpstart sales of your new item. You may also want to time the launch of new items around relevant equestrian events or national holidays, such as the Kentucky Derby or Mother's Day.

There are numerous different methods of creating an energetic product launch. Your product launch depends on your horse business, where your customers find you, the price of the product, and other factors. The following is one sample way to effectuate your product launch:

Promote on your blog and social media sites that your free offer for subscribing is expiring, is being taken down, or will be replaced in the next few days. Make an effort to push your readers to become subscribers during this time.

You can then have a three tier approach to launching your product, using more or less of these tactics based on your business: prompting your email list to buy, using paid advertisements to prompt viewers to buy, and using cross-promotion and affiliate tactics to prompt an audience to buy.

Both physical and online horse businesses can share tactics for the launch of a product or service. If your business exclusively serves a local community market then I would encourage using traditional methods of promoting your new services and products in the community. Use the principles of cross-promotion and affiliate marketing, though with other local people and horse businesses. You can cross-promote your new summer riding camp program for youth with local parents' groups, local elementary schools, the pony club and girl scouts that are in your vicinity. Tell these organizations the value you provide to their audience and they will likely be happy to include you in their newsletter. You can also offer affiliate incentives for local businesses who direct a new customer to you.

ACTION STEP: plan the steps for your new horse product or service launch four weeks in advance of the launch date. Each week reach out to two or three new cross-promoters or affiliates, two weeks in advance notify your audience, readership, or current customers of the upcoming launch. Create an incentive to the early purchasers of your new offering.

ELEVEN: HOW DO I TIE TECHNOLOGY TOGETHER?

There is a lot of technology to consider utilizing in your horse business. Not only do you need to consider your bookkeeping software and electronic billing options, but there are also dozens of social media platforms, e-mail services, web hosting, video hosting and streaming, blogging platforms, and more. The best plan of action is to only use the technology that is vital to creating and sharing your horse business with customers.

There are tools that can schedule your posts in advance and then send those posts out to your various social media sites. However, the number of people who see these posts drop because certain social media platform search tools do not favor programmed posts. Furthermore, many users are finding it disingenuous of a company to blast out the same information on all the different sites. If you choose to have your business profile on any social media sites (as I believe you should), then you should engage with each of those sites in a unique way. Twitter favors a certain type of post that is different than what you would post to LinkedIn, which is different than what you would post to Instagram or Facebook.

It is great if you enjoy using all of these sites and find them productive for your business. In general, I think the number of online outlets is overwhelming for the small business owner. Until you can hire a social media marketing manager, just running the day to day of your business can be fully consuming, and leave you with little time to explore and engage with all your social media profiles. Because of this you should focus on the platforms where your clients are most likely to be found.

Go to your Clients

Certain demographics gravitate towards certain platforms, some platforms are better for follower engagement, and other platforms are best for converting to product sales. Below is a list of some of the most popular social media sites with one or two highlights that can help you narrow down the platforms where you should spend more or less of your effort based on your ideal client, and based on your unique horse business goals. If you are looking to find women in a particular age bracket, then you need to go to the platform where you will find those women. If you are looking to network with other industry leaders who through relationship with you will help promote your business offerings, then be active on the platforms where you will find those colleagues.

Twitter: short snippets of information. This platform works well for re-tweeting content, a valuable way for your content or tweet to be shared many times.

Pinterest: image driven platform. Pinterest is a social media site with one of the highest conversion rates for sales of products. It is increasingly also very valuable for service-based businesses. An excellent image can easily become 'viral' and be shared across many members' boards.

Facebook: great for engaging with your customers. It is easy to generate conversation among your page fans in relation to your photo or text posts. Facebook paid advertising is expensive, but when done right, is proven to have a very high return on investment.

LinkedIn: traditionally used by those in the business world. Joining niche groups is a highly effective way of building your network, particularly with other business owners, entrepreneurs, and horse professionals.

Instagram: an exclusively image-driven site. Some businesses have found great success in sales by posting images related to the business, or behind the scenes of the business.

Google Plus: favored in search results by the search engine and email giant Google. There are niche groups to join, including where you would find both business networking and potential customers.

If you choose to use a social media platform, know the reasons why you are choosing this particular platform.

In my horse business social media use I was hesitant to engage in any platform that I would not be able to use consistently and authentically. Personally I find it disingenuous to use a technology tool that shotgun sprays the same post to all the same sites (though scheduling posts in advance that are specifically tailored to the platform can be very helpful). If you choose to use a social media platform, know the reasons *why* you are choosing this particular platform. If your horse business lends itself to beautiful images, then you know image websites will be effective for you. If your horse business is knowledge-based, then sharing 5-10 valuable and succinct advice tweets a day to your Twitter followers would be effective for your business. Personally, I find LinkedIn to be most helpful for professional networking and Facebook for building a personal relationship with potential customers. I have recently found Pinterest to have growing potential for my business purpose, and find that Twitter helps me gather a wider-base of exposure across equestrian disciplines and business types.

ACTION STEP: Assess the social media sites that you have. Specify the exact business purpose you have in belonging to that site (i.e., networking, advertising, branding) and take three steps this week to make that platform more effective for your business purpose. For example, if you wish to make more product sales of your custom brow bands from Pinterest: 1. take 5 unique pictures of the brow bands in a way that you have not shown them before, 2. re-pin 10 other brow bands on Pinterest that you like to your boards, and 3. create a board that is not about brow bands, but represents the feeling and mission of your personal business brand. Finally, make sure your social media platform clearly displays your website or landing page URL in as many places as possible, such as in captions to photos and in the about section.

TWELVE: WHAT ARE CREATIVE WAYS TO DRIVE SALES?

Sales are the bedrock of your business, because as we have said before, a business is merely a time-consuming hobby if it is not generating income, and generating income requires sales. Whether you have been in the horse business for many years and need a new way to inspire your audience to buy your service or product, or whether you don't know how to increase your sales outside of your current methods, finding creative ways to drive sales can help expand your audience reach and increase your profits. A large part of driving sales is to spend effort in improving your sales funnel, as discussed previously. This section is intended to supplement the sales funnel discussion, and to perhaps inspire you to think of where your sales funnel could benefit from a slightly different approach.

You should never engage in a sales tactic that feel inauthentic to you and your business brand.

As a word of warning, any creativity used in your sales process should be appropriate for your horse business and your target market. A sales process that isolates your target audience would be counterintuitive to your efforts. Finally, you should never engage in a sales tactic that feel inauthentic to you and your business brand. Short of wearing a horse head mask and standing on the corner leading to your Stable waving an oversized arrow with "HORSE LESSONS" printed on it, the following are some methods to drive additional sales that are suitable for both products and services, whether an online or physical business.

-Limited time/ short term offers. This gives rise to a sense of imminence or urgency. Do not overuse this tool, otherwise your customers will be trained to just wait for the next deal.

-Collaborate with other types of businesses. Create joint sales efforts, such as by creating a packaged deal between complementary products and services. For example, you can offer your online horse training course in conjunction with another business person who offers online horse student training courses. Or if you offer a horse training course in one discipline, consider working jointly with another business to add to the training package training videos in a different discipline, in ground manners, or in basic horse tricks! Take the time to consider what your ideal client would be excited to see packaged together or would find to be a helpful service or product when he or she buys from your company. If you sell ground training books or courses, perhaps bundling your product with a training halter from another company would make a great gifting set for the holidays. As an advance warning, if there will be profit-splitting between the two companies, be sure to have the risk of profit and loss allocated between the businesses and get your agreement in writing! *Equine Law Anncouncement:* Your profit and loss sharing may create a legal partnership (even if you don't intend to be partners), and you should consult a business attorney before entering into this type of relationship.

-Offer bonuses. This is a great way to clear surplus horse products that you might have in your business, while also helping the customer feel he or she has gotten a great amount of value for the price. If you sell horse halters but you have a surplus of purple halters, then offer a buy one, get one purple halter half off (or free) sale. This works with lesson packages as well: buy one lesson package, receive horse grooming free, or receive a second lesson package half-off.

-Try a different sales format. If you typically generate buzz and interest for an upcoming promotion or sale in one medium, try adding another. For example, if you have an e-mail sequence to promote a new product or service, try using an image to convey the offering, and also try using it on different platforms where you can find your ideal client. If your traditional method of offering your products has become stale, consider how you can re-introduce it to your ideal client to re-energize and interest your readers and followers. For example, videos, webinars, and podcasts are growing rapidly as ways to help build customer trust. If you have a product business, either post behind the scenes short videos to your appropriate platform, or a beautiful short video that acts as a commercial for your brand. Particularly in the online marketplace, creativity and originality are demanded by a social media saturated world.

-Affiliate. There are many different ways to work with an affiliate, someone who helps promote your product. You can enter into an authentic cross-promotion relationship where you will each help promote each other. You can offer payment or another form of value for those who will promote your product on their platform. There are also specific third party programs that track the number of clicks received on an affiliate's link, and the affiliate is then compensated per click, or per sale, through the affiliate's individual link. Of course, offering another relevant horse businesses' product or service as part of a package with yours will also help expand your audience and prospective customer reach.

ACTION STEP: Consider your number one best method of sales, the number one under-performing method of sales, and one untapped method of sales. Decide how you can further grow the sales through your best method, whether you should stop using your under-performing method of sales or how you can improve that channel, and consider how else your ideal customer would want to shop for your horse product or service. For example, if you have a horse product business your best method of sales may through your business Pinterest page where you have beautiful images of your products, and you might be able to improve sales by creating a seasonal look-book. Your most under-performing method of sales may be Facebook advertising, and you may need to hire a Facebook advertising expert to analyze your analytics, or you may want to cease your Facebook advertising. And your untapped method of sales may be through an e-mail sequence that entices buyers to make a purchase based on your limited-time offers or discounts.

THIRTEEN: BRAND AND MESSAGE, CONNECTING WHAT I HAVE TO WHAT THE MARKET NEEDS

Your brand is the foundation and the driving force behind everything your horse business represents and the mission it strives to accomplish. Your brand is what comes first when developing and growing your horse business, but it is placed in this final section because your brand and message is the accumulation of the education and Action Steps contained earlier in this Guide. Your brand arises from your clear vision of the purpose of your horse business and a careful evaluation of the ideal customer.

There are a number of different formulas to prompt an understanding of your vision and purpose for your horse business. Ultimately the clear articulation of your business vision requires careful thought and reflection, and likely insight from other business owners and mentors who can provide trusted feedback. The following three questions are a solid basis for creating the brand statement of your business. Answer each individually:

1. What problem are you solving for your potential customer? Are you addressing a fear that they have, a want or a need?
2. How do you believe you can solve that problem, fear, want, or need?
3. What topic or interest do you love to engage in?

Establishing your business vision is important for the online or physical business, services or products, and serious or fun. For example, if you sell original horse comics and your goal is to create a series of horse comic books and sell them in every major tack retailer in your country, your vision may be:

1. My customers like to indulge in the whimsical and the humorous, and because my customers love horses, they want great horse comics. Horse comic brands like Thelwell have such staying power because we all need to laugh at ourselves and our horses a little bit more in life.
2. I can provide original, beautiful, and hilarious horse comics that are relatable to every horse person.
3. I love everything about horses, I love creating high-quality pencil sketches, and I particularly love humor about cow ponies and the cutting sport more than anything.

Or, you may have a business vision that delves deeply into the seriousness of human psychology. If your goal is to develop training tools for riders in recovery from a traumatic horse accident, your vision may be:

1. My ideal customer is someone who fears getting back on a horse, and this fear affects other areas of his/her life. My

ideal customer also has the desire to overcome the fear.

2. I can help solve that problem with my special ability and skill in providing tools to recognize and push through the fear. My personality type, my understanding of the horse world, and my training are directly applicable to a successful recovery program for riders.

3. I am an equestrian and a compassionate person trained in psychology. I love the human mind, I love to spend my time learning more about healing of the mind and soul after a traumatic injury, particularly in the context of horses.

After you have worked through these three questions, do it twice more and write a slightly different response to each one. Think of a different angle of the customer problem or desire and how your product or service specifically addresses that customer, and how your horse business is different from your competitors. Never devalue your vision or what you uniquely offer to your ideal customer. For example, if you produce beautiful equestrian scarves or purses, you are providing the customer with new options for high-quality and unique horse accessories.

Once you have established your personal vision and goal for your horse business, you need to translate your vision into your brand visual. Write down the descriptive words that describe your horse business. Words such as elegant, comical, practical, sturdy, or helpful can help you clarify what your website, logo, and color scheme should reflect. Take these descriptive words to a graphic designer if you are not comfortable creating your own design. Graphic designers can be instrumental in developing your brand image, and putting into visual the thoughts that are in your head. If you have the budget, public relations firms or branding companies can help identify your market, define your vision with visuals, and offer other expert advice from their experience. But if you are a small business with a limited budget you can effectively promote your business brand by developing your clear and concise vision (i.e., try to stick to only 5 words in your company's tagline).

A brand is far more than just a single logo. A brand needs to inspire recognition among your audience and loyalty among your clients and customers. A solo horse training business needs to create a brand just as much as an e-commerce horse product business. Whatever the size or type of your business you need to confidently claim your bran, and you must do this to persuade customer's to buy. If you sell horses your brand may be, "My stable has a large selection of sale horses of every experience level and a price point for every budget." Or perhaps, "My stable prides itself on the highest levels of horse sale transparency and ethics." You can then outline on your website HOW you maintain your high level of transparency and ethics, such as vet checks, signed paper documentation, disclosures, and satisfied and repeat customers.

If your brand message is strong and consistent, you are then in control of how your audience talks about your business with others.

Your brand is the opportunity you have to set yourself apart from the competition. To let your prospective customers know why your business is the right horse business for them to find what they are looking for, so that they feel a sense of relief or security to spend their money on your products or services. "I am so glad I found you" are some of the best words a business owner can ever hear. And this perfect match between customer and business derives from the customer's resonance with the business brand.

Realize and articulate the value your business offers to customers. Ensure that this message is reflected in every aspect of your business: your website, your business card, and your customer service with your customers or clients. If your brand message is strong and consistent, you are then in control of how your audience talks about your business with others. What is the first thing people think when they come across your product or services? Is that the message you want them to think? Certain stores are known for generous return policies, other stores are known for unique and high quality products. You are in control of what your horse business will be known for, so go out and share your refined and focused vision, which is your brand, with your audience and your ideal customer will be sure to follow.

Action Step: Regardless of the amount of time you have been in business, outline again the three steps to articulate the financially viable vision you have for your horse business. Ask 3 people whether they feel your current logo, website, and services or product reflect that vision.

Wrapping it all up

Starting and growing a business around your passion can have many highs and lows. There will be mornings you wake up excited to develop your latest equestrian service or product, but there may also be mornings, afternoons, and weekends that you dread certain aspects of growing a horse business. The amount to do can be overwhelming, and running a business online can feel isolating at times. Having a plan of developing your business, growing your business, and receiving support and feedback will be crucial to your horse business success.

Equestrians are a special crowd. As an equestrian you are building a business that offers a unique product or service to your market. And your targeted horse market has its own unique preferences and character. Selling to English riders rather than Western riders can have a dramatically different approach, but at the same time, the two riding styles also have many shared characteristics to which your horse business can deliberately and creatively appeal. **These Action Steps to success begin and end on the foundation of passionately living and breathing your product.** If you sell to horse people, your love and passion for horses and riding will shine through every word and image of your company branding, of your communication with customers, and in the horse products and services you offer.

Wishing you the best of luck and fortitude in implementing the Action Steps. Join our vibrant and ongoing conversation about all things horse business on the blog, RibbonsandRedTape.blogspot.com!

Author Bio

Corinna Charlton is an attorney serving clients in equine legal matters, as well as agricultural and land use issues. She is an H-A Traditional graduate of the United States Pony Club, was an intercollegiate polo player, and is currently showing on the hunter/jumper circuit. You can learn more on her "About Me" page at RibbonsandRedTape.blogspot.com.

www.ingramcontent.com/pod-product-compliance
Lightning Source LLC
Chambersburg PA
CBHW051256170526
45165CB00004B/1731